Set 1 · Book 10

Yum, Gum

Written and Illustrated by Graeme Wilkinson

HIGH NOON BOOKS · NOVATO, CALIFORNIA

High Noon Books
20 Leveroni Court
Novato, CA 94949-5746
800-422-7249
HighNoonBooks.com

Copyright © 2021 by High Noon Books.
All rights reserved. Printed in the United States of America.

No part of this publication may be reproduced, stored in a retrieval system, or transmitted, in any form or by any means, electronic, mechanical photocopying, recording, or otherwise, without the prior written permission of the publisher.

ISBN: 978-1-63402-547-8

Print Number
30 29 28 27 26 25 24 23
10 09 08 07

Order Number: # 2537-9

Quot rubs his tum.

Mum has his gum.

Yum, yum gum.

Gum can get big.

Up bobs Quot.

Up, up, up.

His gum pops.

Bump!
Quot hits his bum.

Dump gum.
It is yuk!

Yum, Gum
Set 1 · Book 10

Sprout Helper

WORD LISTS

DECODABLE WORDS

big	dump	hits	pop	up
bobs	get	is	pops	yuk
bum	gum	it	Quot	yum
bump	has	Mum	rubs	
can	his		tum	

IRREGULAR HIGH-FREQUENCY WORDS

No new words.

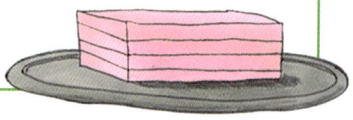

RESPONDING

Who is the story about? (Quot)

Where does Quot live? (in a cave)

What does Quot do to show he's hungry? (He rubs his tum.)

What does Mum give Quot to eat? (gum)

Does Quot like gum? (Yes.) How do you know? (He says "Yum, yum gum.")

What happens after Quot chews the gum? (He blows a big bubble.)

What happens next? (Quot bobs up.)

What makes the bubble pop? (the point of a stalactite on the roof of the cave)

Where does Quot land when he comes down? (on a cactus) What does Quot hurt? (his bum)

In the end, does Quot like gum? (No.) How do you know? (He dumps his gum.)

Do you think gum is good for you? Why or why not? (Answers will vary.)

Note: When answering literal questions, children should show what sentence or picture supports their response.

Little Sprouts

SET 1

SET 1	LIBRARY
Book 1	Pig
Book 2	Mix It!
Book 3	Dex
Book 4	Gus
Book 5	Cat
Book 6	Rat
Book 7	Zak and Yak
Book 8	Fun Run
Book 9	Kev Did It
Book 10	**Yum, Gum**

SET 1 DECODING SKILLS

One-syllable words with:
- ✔ Single consonants
- ✔ Short vowels
- ✔ Consonant /z/ sound spelled *s*
- ✔ Initial and final consonant blends
- ✔ Inflectional ending *–s*